STEP-BY-STEP
Hamburger Magic

STEP-BY-STEP
Hamburger Magic

Jenny Stacey
Photographs by James Duncan

ANNESS PUBLISHING

For my husband, Steve,
and mother, Joy,
with much love and thanks

Produced by Anness Publishing Limited
1 Boundary Row
London SE1 8HP

Publisher: Joanna Lorenz
Editor: Joanne Rippin
Designer: Peter Laws
Jacket Designer: Peter Butler
Photographer: James Duncan
Assistant Home Economist: Elizabeth Silver

Printed and bound in Hong Kong

CONTENTS

INTRODUCTION

Ground meat, particularly beef, has long been a part of our diet. Today, a wider variety of prepared ground meats, such as turkey, chicken, pork and lamb, is readily available in supermarkets and butchers, which has opened the door to a vast range of both simple and more unusual recipes for us to cook at home.

Ground meat may be used extensively, both for the traditional recipes we have come to know and love, or in more exotic foreign recipes, and in quick and easy dishes when time is of the essence. Full of protein, ground meat may be bought in different states, the economical meat being of poorer quality and of a lower nutritional standard. Where possible, the extra lean ground meats should be purchased as these contain less fat and are of a higher quality, which results in a better and much healthier end product.

Ground meat is an excellent basic food to which many different flavorings may be added, making it stretch a little further for more economical cooking. Traditionally used for burgers and chili con carne, ground meat has many other exciting uses. It may be served in pies, or with pasta, rice or noodles, to name but a few, to produce filling and nutritious family meals.

If using a meat grinder or food processor, fish, shellfish and other meats not commercially sold ground may be put through the machine and used in imaginative ways to create wonderful and innovative recipes. When using this book you really will become aware of the versatility of ground meat, and its endless potential as a base for many exciting and flavorful dishes.

Equipment

When using ground meat a bare minimum of basic equipment is required which may be found in the majority of kitchens.

Casserole dish
A covered casserole dish is a must to produce some of the dishes in the book. The lid not only seals in the flavor, but prevents the food from drying out during cooking.

Chopping boards
Nylon chopping boards are recommended for use as they do not hold flavors and are more hygienic. They must be disinfected so that the cuts do not harbor germs.

Colanders
Used for draining large quantities of food.

Cutters
For stamping out shapes and for making croutes.

Garlic press
The best way to add garlic to ground meat recipes.

Grater
For grating cheeses and vegetables for addition to the recipes.

Knives
A set of good cooking knives is essential for chopping ingredients to add to the recipes.

Loaf pan
Used to make meatloaf, this pan is easy to use as it has collapsable sides, making turning out easy.

Grinder
Used to grind raw or cooked meat for use in ground meat recipes, providing the correct textured meat.

Mixing bowls
A variety of sizes are useful for mixing ingredients.

Pastry brush
For brushing and glazing pastry with beaten egg and oiling and greasing baking trays and dishes.

Patty pans
Used for Popovers, these individual sized pans are ideal for producing small portions for children.

Spoons
Essential to cooking, these plastic spoons do not absorb flavors or germs, making them more hygienic than wooden spoons. Used to stir sauces and recipes, during cooking.

Thermometer
Essential for checking the correct cooking temperatures when deep-frying ground meat recipes and not using a deep-fat fryer.

From top left: *colander; loaf pan; sieves; casserole dish; mixing bowls; thermometer; grater; on the patty pans – knives; pastry brush; spoon; on the white chopping board – cutters; grinder; garlic press and salt and pepper mills.*

Herbs

Herbs, both dried and fresh, can be used to enhance the flavor of ground meat dishes. Certain herbs have an affinity with specific foods, eg, dill and fish, basil and tomatoes.

oregano

parsley

tarragon

chives

thyme

basil

rosemary

Basil
There are several types of basil, varying in color and flavor. Basil and tomatoes is a classic combination used for spaghetti sauces, soups, stews and rice dishes.

Chives
Rich in vitamins A and C and a member of the onion family, they are added to dishes for color and flavor. Mainly used in salads, soups and sauces. Long cooking reduces the flavor. This herb adds taste and is used for simple presentation.

Dill
Both the seeds and leaves are very useful for cooking. Each have a distinctive taste. The leaves are added to soft cheeses, seafood, salads and meat sauces.

Oregano
Has a close affinity with marjoram, marjoram being the more delicate flavor. Used for pizza flavoring, salad dressings, in Greek dishes and many other ground meat dishes. Excellent in tomato sauces, marjoram and oregano are best used fresh rather than dried for a better flavor.

Parsley
Both curly and Italian parsley are rich in vitamins and minerals. Used in omelettes, for garnishes, soups, vegetable dishes, mixed with soft cheeses, eggs, sauces and ground meat.

Rosemary
An aromatic herb with a pungent strong flavor. Excellent in jams and jellies and particularly good with lamb and other meats.

Tarragon
Has a subtle aniseed flavor. French tarragon is most commonly used mixed with soft cheeses, sauces, chicken, in dressings, poultry, egg dishes and with fish; one of the four *fines herbes*.

Thyme
There are over 100 species of thyme. Thyme blends well with most flavors and other herbs and is used extensively in meat stews. Delicious with sautéed and baked vegetables, it is also added to many stuffings.

Spices

Dried spices are essential ingredients in cooking. Used in small quantities they should be stored in airtight containers to prevent loss of flavor and color.

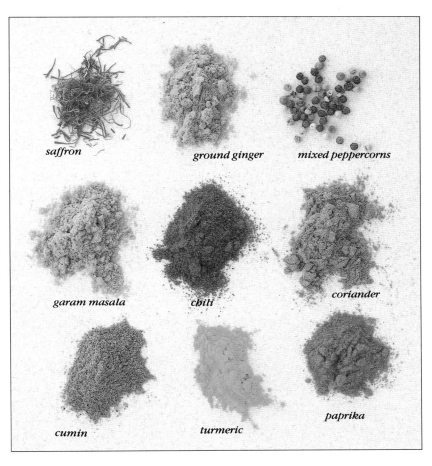

saffron   ground ginger   mixed peppercorns

garam masala   chili   coriander

cumin   turmeric   paprika

Chili

Originating from Mexico, there are many varieties available; such as dried, red, green and yellow. It is a member of the pepper family and has a sweet, fiery and hot taste. It is rich in vitamin C and is used around the world in savory spicy dishes, especially ground meat. The seeds are hot and may be removed before cooking to reduce the heat. Excellent in tomato sauces with meat, beans and lentils. Ground chili powder is a blend of different chilies and spices and is also used in many ground meat dishes.

Coriander

Also available fresh – cilantro, a native of the Middle East with a strong distinctive flavor. Extensively used in curries and spicy dishes, soups and stews.

Cumin

An Eastern spice with a warm distinctive flavor. Very valuable in Indian, Eastern and Mediterranean dishes. Excellent with couscous, curries and stews.

Garam masala

An Indian spice mix of cumin, coriander seeds, cardamom, pepper, cloves and cinnamon. Used extensively in curries and spicy meat dishes.

Ground ginger

Has a fresh spicy flavor and is included in dishes from around the world. Used extensively in oriental cooking, curries and meat dishes.

Mixed peppercorns

Sold as a mixture, these green, black, white and red dried berries of the pepper vine give a hot mixture which when ground into dishes, brings out and enhances flavors.

Paprika

Is ground, sweet peppers. Not usually hot, it adds a tangy rich warmth to meat and vegetable dishes, and a lovely earthy color.

Saffron

Very expensive and therefore used sparingly, it is the stigma from crocuses. It adds a yellow color to dishes and a lovely nutty flavor. Saffron threads are far better than ground saffron. Used extensively with fish, poultry, beef and tomatoes.

Turmeric

A member of the ginger family, it is a Middle Eastern and Indian spice which can be used as a substitute for saffron, but only for color, not for flavor. Adds a mild aroma to many foods.

Kitchen Cupboard

Ground meat is ideal for making use of common kitchen cupboard ingredients to produce quick, tasty meals and snacks.

Barbecue sauce
Is thick in texture and made from fruit, sugar, chili and vinegar. It is brown in color and has an acidic flavor.

Bread crumbs
Can be used both fresh and dried. May be added as a bulking agent in ground meat dishes and used for coating purposes, such as rissoles.

Bulghur wheat or cracked wheat
May be used as a bulking agent in ground meat recipes. Processed from semolina.

Chick peas
Both whole and split, they may be used in casseroles, stuffings and soups. They are available canned or dried, and are used in Middle Eastern recipes.

Chili sauce
Can be mild and very spicy. Made from tomatoes, peppers and spices, it is added to many ground meat recipes.

Cranberry sauce
A condiment traditionally served with turkey, made from cranberries, sugar and vinegar. Excellent for poultry recipes.

Dried apricots
The "no-need-to-soak" variety can be eaten and used from the packet. Excellent with ground lamb, they add a fruity flavor.

Horseradish
The grated root of the horseradish plant, it has a fiery flavor which traditionally complements beef dishes. Made with vinegar and cream it is also ideal with fish.

Kidney beans
Are sweet tasting. Used extensively in Mexican cooking and as a bulking agent for ground meat dishes. They are available canned or dried.

Mayonnaise
Is an emulsion of eggs, oil and lemon. Used in many cold dishes and as a dip.

Mustard
There are many types of mustard available, in both the powdered form and ready-made. Each are blends of different mustard seeds, mixed with vinegar and herbs to give a wide range of flavors and degrees of hotness, the stronger flavors being most suitable with milder foods.

Oatmeal
Rolled oats, ground to varying degrees of fineness. Used as a bulking agent in cooking.

Rice
Used for bulk or as an accompaniment to a meal. Long grain is used the most, mixed with wild rice for a more special dish.

Sesame seeds
Are the seeds of a foreign plant, 50 per cent of which is oil, which is extracted for use in oriental cooking. Has a very distinctive strong nutty flavor. The flavor of sesame seeds can be enhanced by dry roasting and then adding to rice, fish, meat and vegetable dishes.

Soy sauce
Made from soy beans and used extensively in Chinese and Japanese cooking. It enhances the flavor of meat dishes, soups and stews.

Spring roll sauce
A commercially available Chinese sauce, made from tomatoes, chilies and spices. Served with many Chinese recipes or as a dip.

Tomato ketchup
A traditional condiment made from tomatoes, vinegar, sugar and seasoning. Excellent with ground meat.

chick peas

wild rice

kidney beans

horseradish

bread crumbs

sesame seeds

mayonnaise

mustard

ng roll sauce

chili sauce

barbecue sauce

cranberry sauce

rice

tomato ketchup

oatmeal

soy sauce

bulghur wheat

dried apricots

long grain rice

Fresh Ingredients

Many fresh ingredients complement ground meats and fish, adding flavor, color and texture to create a vast range of dishes.

Cheddar cheese
Made from cows' milk. It is available in mild and mature flavors. The sharp version is best used for sauces, and should be grated for melting on toppings.

Chili peppers
May be sweet or hot. They come in a variety of colors and sizes. The sweet pepper has a milder flavor and may be eaten raw. It adds color and flavor to many dishes.

Eggplant
A native to India, the purple eggplant is the most common. It is always eaten cooked and is used in classic ground meat dishes such as moussaka. It has a slightly bitter taste and should be left to stand covered in salt before use to extract the bitter juices.

Gruyère cheese
From Swiss cows' milk. Excellent for melting. It adds a nutty taste to sauces and can be used as a topping.

Leeks
Not as pungent as the onion, but adds a milder flavor and color to main dishes.

Mozzarella cheese
An unripened curd cheese. It melts well and is very suitable for use on pizzas. It has a mild creamy flavor.

Onion
Spanish onions are quite large and both mild and sweet in flavor. They are used extensively in cooking. Red onions are attractive in color and are more oval in shape with a milder, sometimes sweet flavor.

Parmesan cheese
An Italian cheese which is granular and used for grating in cooking. Excellent in sauces. It may also add flavor to dried mixtures.

Rice
A form of carbohydrate, it is used as a bulking agent and served with ground meat dishes such as chili con carne and stroganoff.

Sausages
A wide variety now available, including highly spiced Mediterranean styles. All kinds add flavor to ground meat dishes and their bulk makes the meat extend a little further.

Scallions
Very colorful and mild in taste. Used raw in salads and Chinese cooking to add color and flavor.

Sour cream
A savory cream, soured with lemon juice. Used as a topping and in dips or as an accompaniment to hot dishes.

Spinach
May be used raw in salads or blanched and cooked in dishes. Adds a strong flavor and good color to many ground meat dishes. Combines well with sauces and is full of iron.

Tomatoes
Available all the year round in varying shapes and sizes. Beefsteak tomatoes can be filled with a variety of stuffings, salad tomatoes are excellent for slicing, plum tomatoes are delicious cooked in sauces with ground meat, and cherry tomatoes are good for garnishes.

Yogurt
A product made from curdled milk. It is acidic and less sweet than cream and has far less fat content. Used widely in cooking in sauces or as a topping and for dips.

Techniques

Basic Sauté

This cooking method forms the basis of many ground meat recipes. Meat is cooked in a small amount of oil to tenderize and seal in the flavors.

Dry-frying

An alternative to the basic sauté, dry frying is a healthier way to seal meats as it does not require any additional fat or oil.

1 Heat a little oil in a frying pan for 1 minute.

2 Add the ground meat and sauté gently for 7 minutes.

1 Heat a non-stick frying pan gently over a low flame.

2 Add the ground meat.

3 Stir the meat until brown and sealed.

3 Sauté for 5 minutes, stirring until brown and sealed.

Stir-frying

An increasingly popular cooking method. Foods are quickly fried in a hot wok or heavy-based frying pan with a small amount of oil.

Blanching

This tenderizes foods, cooking them slightly before further use. An ideal way to loosen the skin of tomatoes, nuts etc, making them easier to peel.

1 Heat a wok over a low flame.

2 Add the oil and heat it until almost smoking.

1 Trim the top from the tomatoes and scoop out the central flesh.

2 Bring a pan of water to the boil, add the tomatoes and blanch for 5 minutes.

3 Add the ingredients and fry over a high heat, stirring constantly until cooked through.

3 Remove the tomatoes with a draining spoon, refresh in cold water, and upturn onto a piece of absorbent kitchen paper.

Grinding – with a Food Processor

Foods such as fish and shrimp are ideal for grinding in a food processor, using the chopping blade. A quick method of producing a basic ground meat for recipes.

Grinding – with a Grinder

This is the traditional piece of equipment used to grind both cooked and raw ingredients. There are several different blades with a grinder, allowing different textured grind to be produced.

1 Trim excess fat from the meat and chop into small pieces. Attach the grinder to a work surface and place a bowl underneath. Select the required blade.

1 Wash, skin and bone the fish.

2 Flake the fish and place in a food processor fitted with a chopping blade.

3 Process the fish for 30 seconds on high speed or until finely ground. Use as required.

2 Feed the meat into the top of the grinder, turning the handle all the time. Use the ground meat as required.

Quick Barbecue Sauce

Making use of kitchen cupboard ingredients, this quick relish is ideal for use with burgers, patties and other quick recipes. It has a slightly tangy flavor.

INGREDIENTS
3 tbsp sweet pickle relish
1 tbsp Worcestershire sauce
2 tbsp tomato ketchup
2 tsp prepared mustard
1 tbsp cider vinegar
2 tbsp A-1 Sauce

1 Place the pickle in a bowl.

2 Stir in the Worcestershire sauce, tomato ketchup and prepared mustard.

3 Add the vinegar and A-1 Sauce and mix well. Chill and use as required.

Tomato Sauce

A cooked relish which may be served hot or cold. It has a concentrated tomato flavor, making it ideal with pasta, burgers and many of the snack recipes in the book.

INGREDIENTS
1 tbsp olive oil
1 onion, chopped
1 garlic clove, crushed
2 tbsp flour
2 tbsp tomato ketchup
1¼ cups tomato purée
1 tsp sugar
1 tbsp chopped fresh parsley

1 Heat the oil in a pan. Add the onion and garlic clove and sauté for 5 minutes.

2 Add the flour and cook for 1 minute.

3 Stir in the tomato ketchup, purée, sugar and fresh parsley. Bring to a boil. Chill and use as required.

Chili Sauce

Not for the faint hearted, this is a warm sauce ideal with snacks. For a slightly milder flavor, remove the seeds from the chili before using.

INGREDIENTS
2 large tomatoes
1 red onion
2 tsp chili sauce
1 tbsp chopped fresh basil
1 green chili, chopped
pinch of salt
pinch of sugar

1 Finely chop the tomatoes and place in a mixing bowl.

2 Finely chop the onion and add to the tomatoes with the chili sauce.

3 Stir in the fresh basil, chili, salt and sugar. Use as required.

Cucumber Sauce

A cool, refreshing relish, it may also be used as a dip with such recipes as rissoles, or as a topping on burgers and patties. It should be stored for as short a time as possible.

INGREDIENTS
½ cucumber
2 celery stalks, chopped
1 green bell pepper, seeded and
   chopped
1 garlic clove, crushed
1¼ cups plain yogurt
1 tbsp chopped cilantro
freshly ground black pepper

1 Dice the cucumber and place in a large bowl. Add the celery, green pepper and crushed garlic.

2 Stir in the yogurt and cilantro. Season with the pepper. Cover and chill.

COOK'S TIP

All these sauces should be used as quickly as possible, but will keep for up to a week in the refrigerator.

Basic Bolognese Sauce

A simple, basic recipe which opens the door to many more recipes. Ideal as a pasta sauce or served with rice or baked potatoes.

INGREDIENTS
1 tbsp olive oil
1 tbsp unsalted butter
1 onion, chopped
2 garlic cloves, crushed
1 lb/4 cups ground beef
1 tbsp flour
2 tbsp tomato paste
1¼ cups beef stock
14 oz can chopped tomatoes, with their juice
salt and freshly ground black pepper

1 Heat the oil and butter in a large pan. Add the onion, garlic and ground beef. Cook for 7 minutes stirring all the time, until browned and sealed.

2 Stir in the flour and cook for a further minute. Add the tomato paste.

3 Stir in the stock and canned tomatoes and season well. Use to make one of the variations (right), or cook over a low heat for 50 minutes.

Chili Bean Bolognese Sauce

Making use of the basic sauce, this recipe shows the versatility of ground meat. Spiced with chili powder it has a warm flavor and may be used in Mexican dishes.

INGREDIENTS
1 × basic recipe Basic Bolognese Sauce (left)
1 × 7 oz can red kidney beans, drained
1 × 7 oz can black-eyed peas, drained
1 red chili, sliced
2 oz baby corn, halved
1 tsp chili powder
1 tbsp chopped fresh parsley
salt and freshly ground black pepper

1 Make up the Basic Bolognese Sauce. Add the kidney and black-eyed peas, then stir in the red chili.

2 Add the chili powder, then stir in the corn and cook over a low heat for 50 minutes.

3 Stir in the fresh parsley. Season and use as required.

Vegetable Bolognese Sauce

For those who like a little crunch in their meals, this dish is ideal. The vegetables add color and flavor to the basic sauce, making a suitable filling for lasagne or cannelloni.

INGREDIENTS

1 × basic recipe Basic Bolognese
   Sauce (opposite)
1 carrot
2 celery stalks
1 zucchini
1 green bell pepper
⅓ cup sun-dried tomatoes
2 oz small broccoli florets

1 Make up the Basic Bolognese Sauce. Dice the carrot and add to the sauce.

2 Chop the celery stalks and zucchini and stir into the sauce.

3 Seed and dice the green pepper and chop the sun-dried tomatoes. Add to the sauce together with the broccoli florets. Stir well and cook for 50 minutes. Use as required.

Mushroom and Bacon Bolognese Sauce

This sauce has a smoky flavor. Great with rice or as the basis for a casserole or ground beef pie.

INGREDIENTS

1 × basic recipe Basic Bolognese
   Sauce (opposite)
4 rashers bacon
2 oz smoked sausage
2 large mushrooms
1 tbsp chopped fresh oregano

1 Make up the Basic Bolognese Sauce. Cut the bacon into strips. Stir into the sauce.

2 Slice the sausage, add to the sauce and cook on a low heat for 40 minutes.

3 Peel and slice the mushrooms and add to the sauce together with the fresh oregano. Cook for a further 10 minutes. Use as required.

Dim Sum

Popular as a Chinese snack, these tiny dumplings are fast becoming fashionable in many elegant restaurants.

Serves 4

INGREDIENTS
FOR THE DOUGH
1 ¼ cup flour
¼ cup boiling water
⅛ cup cold water
½ tbsp vegetable oil

FOR THE FILLING
¾ cup ground pork
3 tbsp chopped canned bamboo
    shoots
½ tbsp light soy sauce
1 tsp dry sherry
1 tsp raw sugar
½ tsp sesame oil
1 tsp cornstarch
lettuce leaves such as iceberg, frisée
    or Boston

raw sugar

ground pork

soy sauce

dry sherry

flour

sesame oil

1 For the dough, sift the flour into a bowl. Stir in the boiling water, then the cold water together with the oil. Mix to form a dough and knead until smooth.

2 Divide the mixture into sixteen equal pieces and shape into circles.

3 For the filling, mix together the pork, soy sauce, sherry, sugar and oil.

4 Stir in the cornstarch.

5 Place a little of the filling in the center of each dim sum circle. Pinch the edges of the dough together to form little "pockets."

6 Line a steamer with a damp dish towel. Place the dim sum in the steamer and steam for 5–10 minutes. Serve on a bed of lettuce with soy sauce, scallion curls, sliced red chili and shrimp crackers.

VARIATION

Substitute the pork with cooked peeled shrimp. Sprinkle 1 tbsp of sesame seeds onto the dim sum before cooking.

Beef Chili Soup

A hearty dish based on a traditional chili recipe. Ideal with fresh crusty bread as a warming start to any meal.

Serves 4

INGREDIENTS
1 tbsp oil
1 onion, chopped
1½ cups ground beef
2 garlic cloves, chopped
1 red chili, sliced
2 tbsp flour
1 × 14 oz can chopped tomatoes
2½ cups beef stock
2 cups canned kidney beans,
    drained
2 tbsp chopped fresh parsley
salt and freshly ground black pepper

flour

kidney beans

onion

garlic

parsley

canned tomato

chili

ground beef

1 Heat the oil in a large saucepan. Fry the onion and ground beef for 5 minutes until brown and sealed.

2 Add the garlic, chili and flour. Cook for 1 minute. Add the tomatoes and pour in the stock. Bring to a boil.

COOK'S TIP

For a milder flavor, remove the seeds from the chili after slicing.

3 Stir in the kidney beans and season well. Cook for 20 minutes.

4 Add the fresh parsley and season to taste. Serve with crusty bread.

Samosas

A variation on a popular Indian starter, these golden samosas have a spicy meat and vegetable filling. Delicious served with traditional accompaniments.

Serves 4

INGREDIENTS
1 tbsp oil
1 cup ground beef
3 scallions, sliced
2 oz baby corn, chopped
1 carrot, diced
½ tsp ground cumin
½ tsp ground coriander
1 tsp curry paste
¼ cup beef stock
6 sheets filo pastry
2 tbsp melted butter
oil for deep-frying
fresh cilantro to garnish
lime slices, to garnish
pickle, to serve

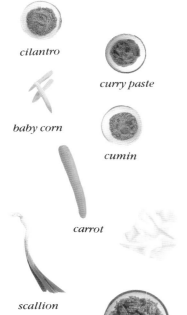

cilantro

curry paste

baby corn

cumin

carrot

scallion

filo pastry

ground beef

1 Heat the oil in a frying pan. Fry the ground beef for 5 minutes until brown and sealed.

2 Add the scallions, corn, carrot, cumin, coriander and curry paste. Cook for a further 5 minutes. Add the stock and bring to a boil.

3 Cut each filo sheet into eight. Brush one piece of pastry with melted butter and lay another sheet on top. Brush with butter and repeat to make eight stacks of pastry. Place one-eighth of the filling in the centre of each square of pastry and brush the pastry edges with butter. Fold into a triangle. Brush with melted butter.

4 Heat the oil for deep-frying in a large heavy-based pan to 350°F. Cook the samosas for 5 minutes until golden brown. Drain well and garnish with fresh cilantro. Serve with lime slices, pickles and papadums.

Spring Rolls

Traditionally a far Eastern side dish, these spicy stuffed spring rolls can also be steamed as a lighter alternative.

Serves 4

INGREDIENTS
FOR THE FILLING
1 tbsp oil
¾ cup ground beef
1 tbsp flour
1 small red bell pepper, seeded and
    chopped
1 small green bell pepper, seeded and
    chopped
4 oz beansprouts
1 tsp Chinese five-spice powder
1 tbsp light soy sauce
2 oz mushrooms, chopped

FOR THE SPRING ROLL SKINS
¾ cup flour
2 tbsp cornstarch
2 tbsp vegetable oil
1¼ cups water
oil for deep-frying
scallion curls, to garnish

ground beef

pepper

soy sauce

five-spice powder

beansprouts

mushrooms

1 For the filling, heat the oil in a frying pan. Add the ground beef and fry for 3 minutes until brown and sealed.

2 Add the flour, red and green peppers, beansprouts, Chinese five-spice powder, soy sauce and mushrooms. Cook for a further 5 minutes.

3 For the pancakes, mix together the flour and cornstarch. Gradually stir in the oil and water to make a smooth batter.

4 Heat a lightly-oiled 6 in omelette pan. Cook one-eighth of the mixture for 2–3 minutes until cooked through. Repeat with the remaining batter, covering the pancakes with a damp dish towel.

5 Place one-eighth of the filling in the center of each pancake, fold in the ends to encase and roll up.

6 Heat the oil for deep-frying in a large heavy-based pan to 350°F. Fry the spring rolls one at a time, for 4–5 minutes. Drain and repeat with the remaining spring rolls. Garnish with scallion curls and serve with soy sauce and lettuce leaves.

Dolmades

These dainty grape leaf parcels are very popular in Mediterranean countries. They are traditionally served as part of a Greek *mezze*.

Serves 4

INGREDIENTS
8 vine leaves

FOR THE FILLING
1 tbsp olive oil
1 cup ground beef
2 tbsp pine nuts
1 onion, chopped
1 tbsp chopped fresh cilantro
1 tsp ground cumin
1 tbsp tomato paste
salt and freshly ground black pepper

FOR THE TOMATO SAUCE
⅔ cup tomato purée
⅔ cup beef stock
2 tsp sugar

grape leaves

cumin

tomato paste

onion

pine nuts

cilantro

ground beef

1 For the filling, heat the oil in a pan. Add the ground beef, pine nuts and onion. Cook for 5 minutes until brown and sealed.

2 Stir in the fresh cilantro, cumin and tomato paste. Cook for a further 3 minutes and season well.

COOK'S TIP

If grape leaves are unavailable, use lettuce or cabbage leaves dropped in boiling water until wilted.

3 Lay eight grape leaves shiny side down on a work surface. Place some of the filling in the center of each leaf and fold the stalk end over the filling. Roll up the parcel towards the tip of the leaf and place in a lightly greased flameproof casserole dish, seam side down.

4 For the sauce, mix together the pureé, stock and sugar and pour over each grape leaf. Cover and cook on a moderate heat for 3–4 minutes. Reduce the heat and cook for a further 30 minutes. Serve with green and red pepper salad.

Cheese Tartlets

These delicious individual tartlets are seasoned with thyme and leeks and topped with a tangy cheese sauce to excite the palate.

Serves 4

INGREDIENTS
8 oz prepared pie crust pastry

FOR THE FILLING
½ tbsp oil
4 oz/1 cup ground beef
½ tbsp chopped fresh thyme
1 small leek, sliced
salt and freshly ground black pepper
sliced cherry tomatoes, to garnish
fresh parsley, to garnish

FOR THE CHEESE SAUCE
1 tbsp butter
1 tbsp flour
½ cup milk
¼ cup freshly grated sharp Cheddar
    cheese
½ tsp mustard

leek

ground beef

cheese

thyme

butter

pastry

1 Preheat the oven to 375°F. Roll out the pastry and cut to fit four 3 in tartlet pans. Bake blind for 15 minutes.

2 Heat the oil in a large pan and fry the ground beef, fresh thyme and leek for 10 minutes. Season and drain if necessary.

3 For the cheese sauce, melt the butter in a pan. Add the flour and cook for 1 minute. Stir in the milk and grated cheese. Bring to a boil, stirring constantly. Add the mustard and season well.

4 Spoon the meat mixture into the base of the tartlet cases, top with the cheese sauce and cook for 10–15 minutes in the preheated oven. Serve with a crisp green salad.

Mexican Tortillas

A variation on a tortilla, this starter (called *Enfrijolades*) combines all the flavors of Mexico with the beef chili and refried beans. Served with guacamole and salsa, it makes a tasty and colorful dish.

Serves 4

INGREDIENTS
FOR THE TORTILLA
½ cup whole wheat flour
2 tsp lard
¼ cup water

FOR THE BEANS
2 tbsp oil
4 cups canned borlotti or pinto beans, drained
1 onion, chopped
1 tbsp chopped fresh cilantro

FOR THE FILLING
1½ cups ground beef
1 onion, chopped
1 red chili, sliced
½ tsp chili powder
2 garlic cloves, chopped
2 tbsp tomato paste
sour cream, guacamole and salsa, to serve

chili

garlic

borlotti beans

chili powder

lard

ground beef

cilantro

onion

1 For the tortilla, sift the flour into a bowl. Rub in the lard until the mixture resembles bread crumbs. Stir in the water to make a soft dough. Knead on a lightly floured surface and cover with a warm, damp towel and leave for 1 hour.

2 Divide the dough into four equal portions. Shape into balls and flatten with a rolling pin. Heat a large heavy-based frying pan over a moderate flame until hot. Place one portion of tortilla mixture in the pan and cook for 30 seconds. Turn and cook for a further 10 seconds. Cover and keep warm in a low oven. Repeat with the remaining tortillas.

3 For the beans, heat the oil in a large pan and fry them together with the onion for 15 minutes. Mash with a fork and add the fresh cilantro. Cook for a further 10 minutes, adding extra oil if necessary.

4 For the filling, dry-fry the ground beef, onion and chili in a large pan for 3 minutes. Keep stirring all the time.

5 Add the chili powder, garlic cloves and tomato paste. Cook for a further 10 minutes over a low heat.

6 Spoon the beans onto the tortilla and top with the beef chili mixture. Serve with small bowls of sour cream, guacamole and salsa.

Beef Casserole and Dumplings

A traditional English recipe, this delicious casserole is topped with light herb dumplings for a filling and nutritious meal.

Serves 4

INGREDIENTS
1 tbsp oil
4 cups ground beef
16 pearl onions
2 carrots, sliced
2 celery stalks, sliced
2 tbsp flour
2½ cups beef stock
salt and freshly ground black pepper

FOR THE DUMPLINGS
1 cup shredded vegetable
  suet
½ cup flour
1 tbsp chopped fresh parsley
water to mix

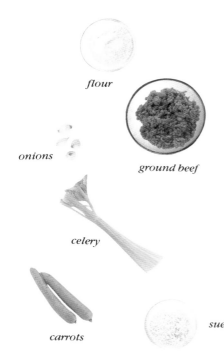

flour

onions

ground beef

celery

carrots

suet

1 Preheat the oven to 350°F. Heat the oil in a flameproof casserole and fry the ground beef for 5 minutes until brown and sealed.

2 Add the onions and fry for 5 minutes, stirring all the time.

3 Stir in the vegetables and flour and cook for a further 1 minute.

4 Add the stock and seasoning. Bring to a boil. Cover and cook in the oven for 1¼ hours.

5 For the dumplings, mix the suet, flour, fresh parsley and water to form a smooth dough.

6 Roll into eight equal-sized balls and place around the top of the casserole for another 20 minutes, uncovered. Serve with broccoli florets.

Coconut Curry

This simple dish makes good use of traditional Indian spices to produce a creamy, flavorful curry with a hint of coconut.

Serves 4

INGREDIENTS
1 tbsp oil
1 lb/4 cups ground beef
2 garlic cloves, chopped
1 tsp ground cumin
1 tsp ground cilantro
1 tsp garam masala
½ in fresh ginger root, chopped
2 tbsp ground almonds
¾ cup coconut milk
½ cup beef stock
2 tbsp chopped fresh cilantro
1 cup long grain rice
1 tsp turmeric
1 tbsp slivered almonds
salt and freshly ground black pepper
fresh cilantro, to garnish
cream, to garnish

1 Heat the oil in a frying pan and fry the ground beef and garlic for 5 minutes.

2 Add the cumin, cilantro, garam masala and ginger. Cook for a further 2 minutes.

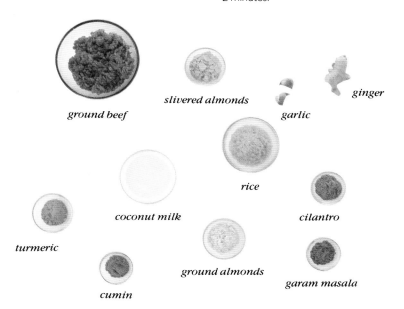

ground beef

slivered almonds

garlic

ginger

rice

cilantro

coconut milk

turmeric

cumin

ground almonds

garam masala

3 Add the ground almonds, season well and stir.

4 Pour in the coconut milk and stock. Mix well and bring to a boil.

COOK'S TIP

If coconut milk is unavailable, grate a block of creamed coconut into a bowl. Pour on boiling water to dissolve, and strain into a bowl.

5 Reduce the heat and simmer for 20 minutes. Stir in the fresh cilantro.

6 Cook the rice in boiling salted water for 10–12 minutes or until *al dente*. Drain well. Return to the pan and stir in the turmeric and slivered almonds. Serve with the coconut curry and garnish with cilantro, cream and ground almonds.

Surf and Turf

Originally made with steak, this simple interpretation will delight the eyes and the palate.

Serves 4

INGREDIENTS
FOR THE GROUND BEEF PATTIES
8 oz/2 cups ground beef
2 cups fresh whole wheat bread
    crumbs
4 scallions, sliced
1 garlic clove, crushed
1 tsp chili powder
2 tbsp oil
salt and freshly ground black pepper

FOR THE SAUCE
2 tbsp flour
⅔ cup dry white wine
¼ cup vegetable stock
½ cup heavy cream
½ cup jumbo shrimp

FOR THE CROUTES
4 slices white bread
2 tbsp butter

garlic

bread

shrimp

ground beef

bread crumbs

flour

butter

chili powder

scallions

1 For the patties, mix the ground beef with the bread crumbs, scallions, garlic clove and chili powder. Season well and form into four equal rounds.

2 Heat the oil in a frying pan and cook the patties for about 7 minutes turning them frequently.

3 For the sauce, add the flour to the frying pan and cook for 1 minute. Gradually pour in the wine, stock, cream and add the shrimp. Cook for 5 more minutes, stirring all the time.

4 For the croutes, stamp out four 10 cm/4 in rounds from the sliced bread. Melt the butter in a frying pan and add the bread. Cook for 2–3 minutes, turning once. Remove and keep warm. Place the patties on the croutes and spoon the sauce over them. Serve with snow peas.

Meatloaf

Another all-American classic, this tasty recipe is given an extra tangy taste with the addition of horseradish sauce.

Serves 4

INGREDIENTS
2 tbsp butter
1 lb/4 cups ground beef
1 onion, chopped
2 garlic cloves, crushed
½ cup bulghur wheat, soaked
¼ cup freshly grated Parmesan
    cheese
1 celery stalk, trimmed and sliced
2 tbsp horseradish sauce
2 tbsp tomato paste
2 tbsp instant oatmeal
1 tbsp chopped fresh thyme
fresh thyme, to garnish

FOR THE SAUCE
2 tbsp horseradish sauce
⅔ cup sour cream

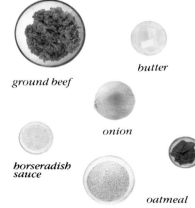

celery

thyme

garlic

butter

ground beef

onion

tomato paste

horseradish sauce

Parmesan cheese

oatmeal

bulghur wheat

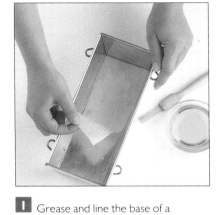

1 Grease and line the base of a 1½ lb loaf pan. Preheat the oven to 350°F.

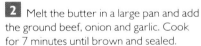

2 Melt the butter in a large pan and add the ground beef, onion and garlic. Cook for 7 minutes until brown and sealed.

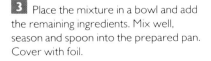

3 Place the mixture in a bowl and add the remaining ingredients. Mix well, season and spoon into the prepared pan. Cover with foil.

4 Stand the loaf pan in a roasting pan and add 1 in of water. Cook in the preheated oven for 1½ hours. Mix together the relish ingredients. Turn out the meatloaf and garnish with fresh thyme. Serve with fresh vegetables.

Moussaka

Once confined to Greece, this simple recipe has fast become a favorite dish in homes and restaurants across the continents.

Serves 4

INGREDIENTS
1 tbsp oil
8 oz/2 cups ground lamb
1 tsp ground cumin
1 red onion, chopped
2 tbsp flour
¾ cup lamb or beef stock
2 tbsp tomato paste
1 tbsp chopped fresh oregano
1 eggplant, sliced
salt and freshly ground black pepper

FOR THE SAUCE
2 tbsp butter
2 tbsp flour
1¼ cups milk
½ cup freshly grated Cheddar cheese
1 egg, beaten

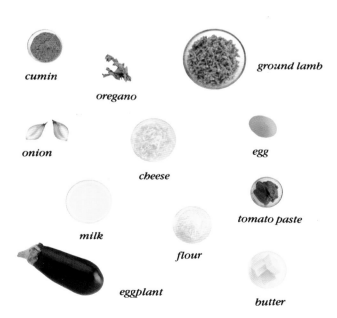

cumin

oregano

onion

cheese

egg

milk

flour

tomato paste

eggplant

butter

ground lamb

1 Preheat the oven to 350°F. Heat the oil in a large pan and fry the lamb and cumin for 5 minutes.

2 Add the onion and fry for a further 5 minutes, stirring occasionally.

3 Add the flour and cook for 1 minute. Stir in the stock, tomato paste and fresh oregano. Bring to a boil. Reduce the heat and cook for 30 minutes.

4 Cover a plate with paper towels. Lay the sliced eggplant on top and sprinkle with salt. Stand for 10 minutes. Rinse thoroughly and pat dry.

VARIATION

If you wish, substitute potatoes for the eggplant. Thinly slice one large potato, parboil, drain and layer into the dish.

5 For the sauce, melt the butter in a pan, add the flour and cook for 1 minute. Gradually stir in the milk and grated cheese, season well and bring to a boil, stirring continuously. Remove from heat and stir in the egg.

6 Spoon the lamb into a dish, lay the eggplant on top and spoon on the sauce. Cook in the preheated oven for 45–60 minutes. Serve with a Greek salad.

Greek Pasta Casserole

Another excellent main meal (called *Pastitsio* in Greece), this recipe is both economical and filling.

Serves 4

INGREDIENTS
1 tbsp oil
1 lb/4 cups ground lamb
1 onion, chopped
2 garlic cloves, crushed
2 tbsp tomato paste
2 tbsp flour
1¼ cups lamb stock
2 large tomatoes
1 cup pasta shapes
2 cups strained plain yogurt
2 eggs
salt and freshly ground black pepper

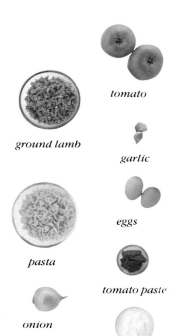

tomato

ground lamb

garlic

eggs

pasta

tomato paste

onion

yogurt

flour

1 Preheat the oven to 375°F. Heat the oil in a large pan and fry the lamb for 5 minutes. Add the onion and garlic and continue to fry for a further 5 minutes.

2 Stir in the tomato paste and flour. Cook for 1 minute.

3 Stir in the stock and season to taste. Bring to a boil and cook for 20 minutes.

4 Slice the tomatoes, place the meat in an ovenproof dish and arrange the tomatoes on top.

5 Cook the pasta shapes in boiling salted water for 8–10 minutes or until *al dente*. Drain well.

6 Mix together the pasta, yogurt and eggs. Spoon on top of the tomatoes and cook in the preheated oven for 1 hour. Serve with a crisp salad.

Beef Ragout

Full of the goodness of vegetables, this recipe is based on the ever-popular couscous recipes of North Africa.

Serves 4

INGREDIENTS
1 tbsp oil
1 lb/4 cups ground beef
1 garlic clove, crushed
1 onion, quartered
2 tbsp flour
⅔ cup dry white wine
⅔ cup beef stock
2 baby turnips, chopped
4 oz rutabaga, chopped
2 carrots, cut into chunks
2 zucchini, cut into chunks
1 tbsp chopped fresh cilantro
5 ml/1 tsp ground coriander
2 cups couscous
salt and freshly ground black pepper
fresh cilantro, to garnish

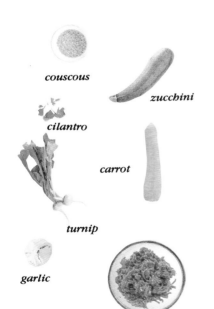

couscous

zucchini

cilantro

carrot

turnip

garlic

ground beef

onion

white wine

rutabaga

1 Heat the oil in a large pan. Add the ground beef and fry for 5 minutes. Add the garlic, and onion. Cook for a further 3 minutes.

2 Stir in the flour and cook for about 1 minute. Add the wine and stock, season and bring to a boil, stirring all the time.

3 Add the vegetables with the cilantro and ground coriander. Reduce the heat, cover and cook for 15 minutes.

4 Meanwhile, place the couscous in a bowl, and cover with boiling water. Leave to stand for 10 minutes. Drain and place in a lined steamer or colander. Remove the lid from the pan and place the steamer on top. Steam the couscous over the pan for a further 30 minutes. Garnish with fresh cilantro and serve.

Beef Braid

This is an attractive alternative to a ground beef pie. The braided pastry contains a flavorful filling and is topped with cheese.

Serves 4

INGREDIENTS
1 tbsp oil
4 cups ground beef
2 leeks, sliced
1 tbsp tomato paste
1 tbsp chopped fresh rosemary
2 tbsp flour
⅔ cup beef stock
1 lb prepared pie crust pastry
2 tbsp freshly grated Cheddar cheese
1 egg, beaten

ground beef   *leek*

pastry

rosemary

cheese

tomato paste

1 Preheat the oven to 375°F. Heat the oil in a large pan, add the ground beef and cook for 5 minutes. Stir in the leeks, tomato paste and fresh rosemary. Season well to taste.

2 Add the flour and cook for 1 minute. Stir in the stock gradually and cook for a further 20 minutes.

3 Roll out the prepared pastry on a lightly floured surface to a large rectangle about 12 × 10 in in size. Place the ground beef mixture in the center of the pastry along the length.

4 Top with the grated cheese. Make parallel diagonal cuts on either side of the filling, fold in each pastry end and then alternate pastry strips. Brush with beaten egg and cook for 40 minutes.

Beef Chili Tortilla

Perhaps the best-known Mexican recipe (called *Chimichanga*), wheat tortillas filled with beef chili are topped with a spicy cheese sauce.

Serves 4

INGREDIENTS
4 wheat tortillas

FOR THE FILLING
1 tbsp olive oil
1 lb/4 cups ground beef
1 onion, chopped
1 tsp paprika
1 red chili, sliced
1 tbsp flour
⅔ cup beef stock
2 large tomatoes
salt and freshly ground black pepper
green bell peppers, chopped
   tomatoes, guacamole, sour cream,
   to serve

FOR THE CHEESE SAUCE
2 tbsp butter
2 tbsp flour
1¼ cups milk
½ cup freshly grated sharp Cheddar
   cheese
pinch of paprika

chili

cheese

tortillas

ground beef

tomatoes

onion

1 Preheat the oven to 350°F. For the filling, heat the oil in a large pan and fry the ground beef for 5 minutes. Add the onion and fry for a further 5 minutes.

2 Add the paprika, chili and flour. Cook for 1 minute.

3 Stir in the stock. Season well and bring to a boil. Reduce the heat and cook for 20 minutes.

4 For the cheese sauce, melt the butter in a pan and add the flour. Cook for 1 minute and stir in the milk. Add the grated cheese and paprika, season to taste and bring to a boil, stirring continuously. Chop the tomatoes.

5 Place a little of the ground beef mixture along the length of each tortilla. Place the tomatoes on top, roll up into a "cigar" shape and place seam side down in an ovenproof dish.

6 Pour the cheese sauce over each tortilla and cook in the preheated oven for 20 minutes. Serve with green peppers, chopped tomato, guacamole and sour cream.

Koftas

A fun way to serve spicy ground lamb. These tasty kebabs are packed with flavors from the Mediterranean.

Serves 4

INGREDIENTS
1 lb/4 cups ground lamb
1½ cups fresh whole wheat bread
   crumbs
1 onion, grated
5 ml/1 tsp ground cumin
2 garlic cloves, crushed
1 egg, beaten
¼ cup lamb stock
salt and freshly ground black pepper

bread crumbs

egg

garlic

cumin

ground lamb

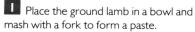
onion

1 Place the ground lamb in a bowl and mash with a fork to form a paste.

2 Add the bread crumbs and onion.

3 Stir in the cumin and garlic. Season well to taste.

4 Stir in the egg and stock with a fork. Using your hands bind the mixture together until smooth.

5 Shape into "sausages" with lightly floured hands.

COOK'S TIP
Soak the wooden skewers in cold water for 30 minutes before using to prevent them from burning.

6 Thread onto wooden kebab skewers and broil under a medium heat for 30 minutes, turning occasionally. Serve with a crisp green salad.

Sandwich Loaves

An interesting variation on a hot sandwich, these individual loaves are a filling snack which may be prepared in advance.

Serves 4

INGREDIENTS
1 tbsp oil
1 cup ground beef
1 tbsp horseradish sauce
1 tsp mustard
2 oz snow peas
1 leek, sliced
1 carrot, cut into strips
4 individual whole wheat loaves
¾ cup ready-to-eat dried apricots, chopped
salt and freshly ground black pepper

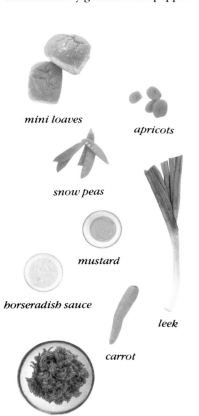

mini loaves

apricots

snow peas

mustard

horseradish sauce

leek

carrot

ground beef

1 Preheat the oven to 375°F. Heat the oil in a large pan and fry the ground beef for around 5 minutes until brown and sealed. Add the horseradish sauce and mustard and season well to taste.

2 Place the vegetables and apricots in a pan of lightly salted boiling water. Cook for 5 minutes and drain.

COOK'S TIP
Reserve the scooped bread and make it into bread crumbs. Freeze for future recipes such as stuffing and burgers.

3 Slice the tops from the loaves and reserve them. Scoop out the center of the loaves, leaving a ½ in shell.

4 Layer the beef, vegetables and apricots into the loaves, packing the ingredients down well. Replace the lid, wrap in foil and cook for 35 minutes in the preheated oven.

Stuffed Tomatoes

Ever popular, this recipe demonstrates the versatility of its use here as a stuffing.

Serves 4

INGREDIENTS
4 large beefsteak tomatoes
½ tbsp oil
3 oz/¾ cup ground beef
1 small red onion, thinly sliced
¼ cup bulghur wheat
2 tbsp freshly grated Parmesan
  cheese
1 tbsp unsalted cashew nuts,
  chopped
1 small celery stalk, chopped
salt and freshly ground black pepper

ground beef

cashew nuts

celery

bulghur wheat

Parmesan cheese

tomato   *onion*

1 Trim the top from the tomatoes, scoop out the flesh with a teaspoon and reserve. Blanch the tomatoes for 2 minutes in boiling water and drain well.

2 Heat the oil in a large pan, add the ground beef and onion, and cook for 10 minutes. Stir in the tomato flesh. Place the bulghur wheat in a bowl, cover with boiling water and leave to soak for 10 minutes. Drain if necessary.

3 Mix the mince and bulghur, grated cheese, nuts and celery. Season well.

4 Spoon the filling into the tomatoes and broil under a medium heat for 10 minutes. Serve with a crisp green salad.

Turkey Crepes

Making good use of the different types of ground meat now available, these quick and easy crepes are filled with a delicious turkey and apple mixture.

Serves 4

INGREDIENTS
FOR THE FILLING
2 tbsp oil
4 cups ground turkey
2 tbsp chopped fresh chives
2 Granny Smith apples, cored and
    diced
2 tbsp flour
¾ cup chicken stock
salt and freshly ground black pepper

FOR THE PANCAKES
1 cup flour
pinch of salt
1 egg, beaten
1¼ cups milk
oil for frying

FOR THE SAUCE
4 tbsp cranberry sauce
¼ cup chicken stock
1 tbsp honey
1 tbsp cornstarch

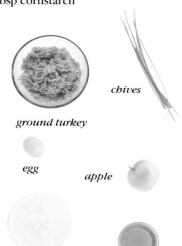

ground turkey

chives

egg

apple

flour

honey

1 For the filling, heat the oil in a large pan and fry the turkey for 5 minutes. Add the chives and apples and then the flour. Stir in the stock and seasoning. Cook for 20 minutes.

2 For the crepes, sift the flour into a bowl with a pinch of salt. Make a well in the center and drop in the egg. Beat it in gradually with the milk to form a smooth batter. Heat the oil in a 6 in omelette pan. Pour off the oil and add one-quarter of the crepe batter. Tilt the pan to cover the base with the mixture and cook for 2–3 minutes. Turn the pancake over and cook for a further 2 minutes. Stack each crepe on top of one another and keep warm.

3 For the sauce, put the cranberry sauce, stock and honey into a pan. Heat gently until melted. Blend the cornstarch with 4 tsp water, stir it in and bring to a boil, stirring until clear.

4 Lay the crepes on a chopping board, spoon the filling into the center and fold over around the filling. Place on a plate and spoon on the sauce. Serve with a fresh vegetable such as snow peas.

Speedy Pizzas

Ever popular as a snack, this pizza really comes into its own for speed and flavor. It uses ready-made muffins as a filling base.

Serves 4

INGREDIENTS
2 muffins

FOR THE TOPPING
2 tsp oil
4 oz/1 cup ground beef
1 small onion, sliced
1 tbsp flour
¼ cup beef stock
1 tbsp tomato paste
½ green bell pepper, chopped
6 pitted black olives, sliced
1 oz mozzarella cheese, sliced
salt and freshly ground black pepper

FOR THE SAUCE
2 tbsp butter
2 tbsp flour
⅔ cup milk
2 tbsp chopped fresh basil

olives

pepper

mozzarella cheese

tomato paste

flour

1 Preheat the oven to 400°F. Heat the oil in a large pan, add the ground beef and cook for 5 minutes. Stir in the onion and cook for a further 3 minutes. Add the flour, stock, tomato paste and pepper. Season well. Cook gently for 7 minutes.

2 For the sauce, melt the butter in a pan, add the flour and cook for 1 minute. Gradually stir in the milk and bring to a boil, add the basil and season to taste.

3 Cut each muffin in half and spoon a little sauce onto each one.

4 Top with the meat mixture, olives and mozzarella cheese. Cook for 10–15 minutes and serve with coleslaw and a crisp green salad.

Croquettes

Ground beef is blended with potato and herbs, coated and fried, to provide an economical and satisfying meal or a tasty starter.

Serves 4

INGREDIENTS
1 lb potatoes, cubed
6 oz/1 ½ cups ground beef
3 scallions, chopped
1 tbsp chopped fresh parsley
1 egg, beaten
1 cup dried whole wheat bread
    crumbs
oil for deep-frying
salt and freshly ground black pepper

FOR THE DIP
½ cup mayonnaise
½ cup plain yogurt
1 tbsp chopped fresh parsley

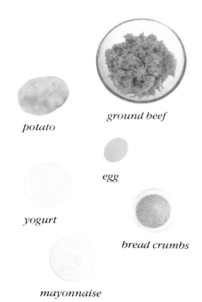

potato

ground beef

egg

yogurt

bread crumbs

mayonnaise

scallion

parsley

1 Cook the potatoes in a pot of lightly salted boiling water for 20 minutes. Drain.

2 Dry-fry the ground beef in a large pan for 5 minutes. Add the scallions and cook for a further 2 minutes.

3 Stir in the fresh parsley and season well to taste.

4 Mash the potatoes and mix into the meat. Roll into eight sausage-shaped croquettes with lightly floured hands.

5 Place the egg in a shallow dish and the bread crumbs in another. Dip the croquettes into the egg to coat them and then roll in the crumbs to cover each one completely.

6 Heat the oil in a large heavy-based pan for deep-frying to 350°F. Cook the croquettes in two batches for 5–7 minutes or until golden. Drain well. Mix the dip ingredients together and serve with cherry tomatoes and lettuce.

Fritters

A variation on beef patties, coated in batter and lightly fried, this tasty alternative need only be served with a light salad to provide a substantial snack.

Serves 4

INGREDIENTS
FOR THE PATTIES
8 oz/2 cups ground beef
1 onion, grated
2 tsp chopped fresh oregano
½ cup canned corn, drained
1 tsp mustard
2 cups fresh white bread crumbs
oil for deep-frying
salt and freshly ground black pepper

FOR THE BATTER
1 cup flour
¼ cup warm water
3 tbsp melted butter
¼ cup cold water
1 egg white

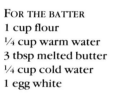

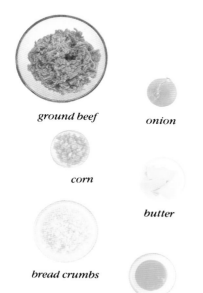

ground beef

corn

bread crumbs

onion

butter

mustard

oregano

1 For the patties, place the ground beef in a bowl and mash with a fork. Add the onion, oregano, corn, mustard and bread crumbs. Season well.

2 Form into eight round patties with lightly floured hands.

3 For the batter, sift the flour into a bowl and stir in the warm water and melted butter. Mix to a smooth batter with the cold water. Whisk the egg white until peaking and fold into the mixture.

4 Heat the oil for deep-frying to 325°F. Dip the patties into the batter to coat and fry two at a time in the oil. Drain on paper towels and serve with tomato pickle and green salad.

Nachos

The addition of beef to this Mexican appetizer makes a hearty meal. Guacomole on the side makes the dish even more delicious.

Serves 4

INGREDIENTS
8 oz/2 cups ground beef
2 red chilies, chopped
3 scallions, chopped
6 oz nachos
1 ¼ cups sour cream
½ cup freshly grated medium-sharp
   Cheddar cheese
salt and freshly ground black pepper

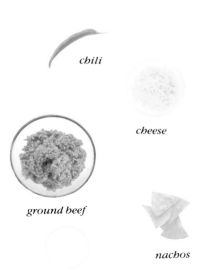

chili

cheese

ground beef

nachos

cream

scallions

1 Dry-fry the ground beef and chilies in a large pan for 10 minutes, stirring all the time.

2 Add the scallions, season and cook for a further 5 minutes.

3 Arrange the nachos in four individual flameproof dishes.

4 Spoon on the ground beef mixture, top with sour cream and grated cheese. Broil under a medium heat for 5 minutes.

Mini Beef Pies

Ever popular, these meat and vegetable filled parcels may be made in advance and frozen.

Serves 8

INGREDIENTS
1 tbsp oil
1 ½ cups ground beef
1 tbsp tomato paste
1 onion, chopped
1 carrot, diced
2 oz turnip, diced
1 large potato, diced
2 tbsp flour
⅔ cup beef stock
1 tbsp chopped fresh parsley
1 lb prepared pie crust pastry
1 egg, beaten
salt and freshly ground black pepper

pastry

egg

tomato paste

ground beef

parsley

onion

turnips

flour

carrot

potato

1 Preheat the oven to 375°F. Heat the oil in a large pan and add the ground beef. Cook for 5 minutes. Stir in the tomato paste, onion, carrot, turnip and potato. Cook for a further 5 minutes.

2 Add the flour and cook for 1 minute. Stir in the stock and season to taste. Cook over a gentle heat for 10 minutes. Stir in the fresh parsley and cool.

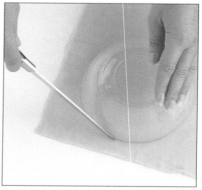

3 Roll out the pastry to a large rectangle. Cut eight 6 in circles.

4 Spoon the filling onto one half of each pastry circle, brush the edges with egg and fold in half to form a semi-circle. Crimp the edges and roll. Brush the pies with egg and place on a baking sheet. Cook for 35 minutes or until golden. Serve with a crisp salad.

Soufflé Omelette

This light omelette requires a deft touch. It should be served immediately after it's prepared to fully appreciate its texture and flavor.

Serves 4

INGREDIENTS
FOR THE FILLING
1 tbsp oil
8 oz/2 cups ground beef
1 onion, quartered
3 tbsp flour
2/3 cup red wine
2/3 cup beef stock
3 rashers hickory-smoked bacon, chopped
1 tsp paprika
1/2 cup freshly grated Gruyère cheese
salt and freshly ground black papper

FOR THE OMELETTE
8 eggs, separated
1/2 cup water
2 tbsp butter

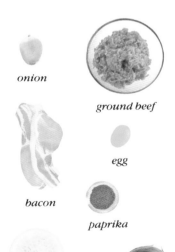

onion

ground beef

egg

bacon

paprika

Gruyère cheese

wine

1 For the filling, heat the oil in a large pan. Add the ground beef and cook for 5 minutes. Stir in the onion and cook for a further 5 minutes. Add the flour and pour in the red wine, stock and bacon. Season to taste and add the paprika. Cook over a low heat while preparing the omelette.

2 Preheat broiler. For the omelette, whisk the egg yolks until creamy. Season to taste and pour in the water and whisk again. Whisk the egg whites until peaking.

3 Melt one-quarter of the butter in a 6 in omelette pan. Fold the egg whites into the yolk mixture and pour one-quarter of the mixture into the pan. Cook for 2–3 minutes until golden brown on the underside.

4 Broil under a medium heat for 2–3 minutes or until browned. Loosen with a spatula and spoon in one-quarter of the grated cheese and one-quarter of the meat filling. Fold over the omelette and serve immediately. Repeat with the remaining filling and omelette mixture. Serve with freshly cooked vegetables.

Stilton Burger

Slightly more up-market than the traditional burger, this tasty recipe contains a delicious surprise. The lightly melted Stilton cheese encased in a crunchy burger is absolutely delicious.

Serves 4

INGREDIENTS
1 lb/4 cups ground beef
1 onion, finely chopped
1 celery stalk, chopped
1 tsp dried mixed herbs
1 tsp prepared mustard
½ cup crumbled Stilton cheese
4 burger buns
salt and freshly ground black pepper

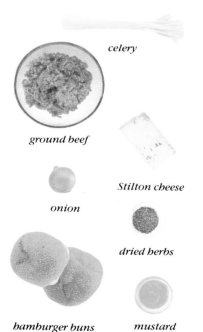

celery

ground beef

Stilton cheese

onion

dried herbs

hamburger buns

mustard

1 Place the ground beef in a bowl together with the onion and celery. Season well.

2 Stir in the herbs and mustard, bringing them together to form a firm mixture.

3 Divide the mixture into eight equal portions. Place four on a chopping board and flatten each one slightly.

4 Place the crumbled cheese in the center of each.

5 Flatten the remaining mixture and place on top. Mold the mixture together encasing the crumbled cheese and shape into four burgers.

6 Grill under a medium heat for 10 minutes, turning once or until cooked through. Split the hamburger buns and place a burger inside each. Serve with salad, ketchup, and mustard pickle.

Spaghetti with Bolognese Sauce

A spicy version of a popular dish. Worcestershire sauce and chorizo sausages add an extra element to this perfect family standby.

Serves 4

INGREDIENTS
1 tbsp oil
8 oz/2 cups ground beef
1 onion, chopped
1 tsp ground chili powder
1 tbsp Worcestershire sauce
2 tbsp flour
2/3 cup beef stock
4 chorizo sausages
2 oz baby corn
1 × 7 oz can chopped tomatoes
1 tbsp chopped fresh basil
salt and freshly ground black pepper

ground beef

basil

canned tomato

chili powder

chorizo

baby corn

Worcestershire sauce

onion

1 Heat the oil in a large pan and fry the ground beef for 5 minutes. Add the onion and chili powder and cook for a further 3 minutes.

2 Stir in the Worcestershire sauce and flour. Cook for 1 minute before pouring in the stock.

COOK'S TIP
Make up the Bolognese sauce and freeze in conveniently sized portions for up to 2 months.

3 Slice the chorizo sausages and halve the corn lengthways.

4 Stir in the sausages, tomatoes, corn and chopped basil. Season and bring to a boil. Reduce the heat and simmer for 30 minutes. Serve with spaghetti, garnished with fresh basil.

Spicy Beef

Promoting a fast-growing trend in worldwide cuisine, the wok is used in this recipe to produce a colorful and healthy meal.

Serves 4

INGREDIENTS

1 tbsp oil
1 lb/4 cups ground beef
1 in fresh ginger root, sliced
1 tsp Chinese five-spice powder
1 red chili, sliced
2 oz snow peas
1 red bell pepper, chopped
1 carrot, sliced
4 oz beansprouts
1 tbsp sesame oil

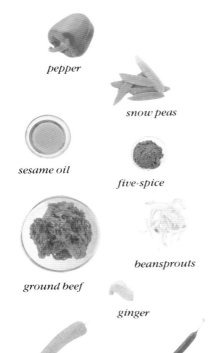

pepper

snow peas

sesame oil

five-spice

beansprouts

ground beef

ginger

carrot

chili

1 Heat the oil in a wok until almost smoking. Add the ground beef and cook for 3 minutes, stirring all the time.

2 Add the ginger, Chinese five-spice powder and chili. Cook for 1 minute.

3 Add the snow peas, pepper and carrot and cook for a further 3 minutes, stirring continuously.

4 Add the beansprouts and sesame oil and cook for a final 2 minutes. Serve immediately with noodles.

Ground Pork Casserole

Ground pork combines with the sweetness of apple and the texture of crunchy vegetables. Covered with an oatmeal topping, this is a meal to tempt the family.

Serves 4

INGREDIENTS
FOR THE FILLING
1 tbsp oil
1 lb/4 cups ground pork
1 onion, sliced
2 tbsp flour
⅔ cup milk
⅔ cup vegetable stock
2 oz broccoli florets
½ cup canned corn, drained
1 Granny Smith apple, cored and
  diced
salt and freshly ground black pepper

FOR THE TOPPING
½ cup instant oatmeal
½ cup flour
1 tbsp butter
¼ cup freshly grated Colby cheese

1 Preheat the oven to 350°F. For the filling, heat the oil in a large pan and fry the pork for 5 minutes. Add the onion and continue to fry for a further 3 minutes.

2 Stir in the flour and cook for 1 minute. Pour in the milk and stock and bring to a boil, stirring all the time.

3 Add the broccoli, corn and apple.

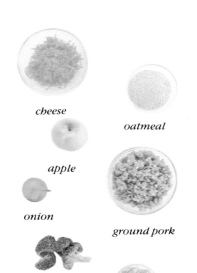

cheese

oatmeal

apple

onion

ground pork

broccoli

corn

4 Spoon the mixture into four individual ovenproof dishes.

5 For the crumble topping, mix together the oatmeal and flour, then rub in the butter.

VARIATION

For a rich cheese topping, mix together crushed potato chips and grated cheese. Cook as before.

6 Spoon the topping onto the pork mixture and press down with the back of a spoon. Scatter over the cheese and place in the pre-heated oven. Cook for 45 minutes. Garnish with slices of apple and serve at once.

Risotto

An Italian dish made with short grain arborio rice
which gives a creamy consistency to this easy
one-pan recipe.

Serves 4

INGREDIENTS
1 tbsp oil
1½ cups arborio rice
1 onion, chopped
8 oz/2 cups ground chicken
2½ cups chicken stock
1 red bell pepper, seeded and
    chopped
1 yellow bell pepper, seeded and
    chopped
3 oz frozen green beans
4 oz cremini mushrooms, sliced
1 tbsp chopped fresh parsley
salt and freshly ground black pepper
fresh parsley, to garnish

green beans

ground chicken

parsley

peppers

cremini mushroom

rice

onion

1 Heat the oil in a large frying pan. Add the rice and cook for 2 minutes until translucent.

2 Add the onion and ground chicken. Cook for 5 minutes, stirring occasionally.

3 Pour in the stock and bring to a boil.

4 Stir in the peppers and reduce the heat. Cook for 10 minutes.

5 Add the green beans and mushrooms and cook for a further 10 minutes.

6 Stir in the fresh parsley and season well to taste. Cook for 10 minutes or until the liquid has been absorbed. Serve, garnished with fresh parsley.

Stuffed Cabbage

An unusual combination of flavors, this recipe incorporates a Middle Eastern filling into a traditional English dish.

Serves 4

INGREDIENTS
1 savoy cabbage
1 tbsp oil
4 oz/1 cup ground beef
1 red onion, chopped
1 tbsp chopped fresh thyme
2 tbsp flour
¼ cup raisins
⅔ cup beef stock
½ cup canned chick peas, rinsed and
   drained
1 tsp garam masala
1 cup fresh whole wheat bread
   crumbs
salt and freshly ground black pepper

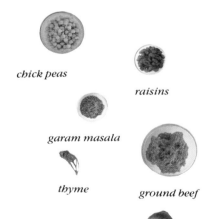

chick peas

raisins

garam masala

thyme   *ground beef*

onion

bread crumbs

cabbage

1 Preheat the oven to 400°F. Remove the outer leaves from the cabbage. Blanch the remaining cabbage in boiling water for 5 minutes. Drain well.

2 Heat the oil in a large pan and fry the ground beef for 5 minutes. Add the onion and the thyme and cook for a further 3 minutes.

3 Stir in the flour and cook for 1 minute. Add the raisins and slowly pour in the stock.

4 Stir in the chickpeas and garam masala. Remove the mixture from the heat and add the bread crumbs. Mix and season well.

5 Trim the top from the cabbage and scoop out the center.

COOK'S TIP
Use the filling to stuff beefsteak tomatoes, cooked eggplant or peppers. Broil under a medium heat for 10–15 minutes.

6 Spoon in the meat mixture, wrap in foil and bake in the preheated oven for 30 minutes. Serve with freshly cooked vegetables.

Cannelloni

This Italian dish has fast become popular, offering many variations to the original recipe. This version introduces a variety of vegetables which are topped with a traditional cheese sauce.

Serves 4

INGREDIENTS
8 cannelloni tubes
4 oz spinach

FOR THE FILLING
1 tbsp oil
1 ½ cups ground beef
2 garlic cloves, crushed
2 tbsp flour
½ cup beef stock
1 small carrot, finely chopped
1 small yellow squash, chopped
salt and freshly ground black pepper

FOR THE SAUCE
2 tbsp butter
2 tbsp flour
1 cup milk
½ cup freshly grated Parmesan
    cheese

spinach

ground beef

cannelloni

garlic

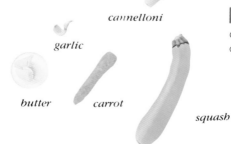

butter   *carrot*

squash

1 Preheat the oven to 350°F. For the filling, heat the oil in a large pan. Add the ground beef and garlic. Cook for 5 minutes.

2 Add the flour and cook for a further 1 minute. Slowly stir in the stock and bring to a boil.

3 Add the carrot and squash, season well and cook for 10 minutes.

4 Spoon the beef mixture into the cannelloni tubes and place in an ovenproof dish.

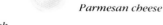

Parmesan cheese

5 Blanch the spinach in boiling water for 3 minutes. Drain well and place on top of the cannelloni tubes.

6 For the sauce melt the butter in a pan. Add the flour and cook for 1 minute. Pour in the milk, add the grated cheese and season well. Bring to a boil, stirring all the time. Pour over the cannelloni and spinach and cook for 30 minutes in the preheated oven. Serve with tomatoes and a crisp green salad.

Chicken in Puff Pastry

A spectacular centerpiece, this light pastry case contains a delicious chicken and mushroom filling with a hint of fruit. Ideal served with freshly cooked vegetables.

Serves 4

INGREDIENTS
1 lb prepared puff pastry
beaten egg

FOR THE FILLING
1 tbsp oil
4 cups ground chicken
2 tbsp flour
⅔ cup milk
⅔ cup chicken stock
4 scallions, chopped
¼ cup red currants
3 oz button mushrooms, sliced
1 tbsp chopped fresh tarragon
salt and freshly ground black pepper

1 Preheat the oven to 400°F. Roll half the pastry out on a lightly floured work surface to a 10 in oval. Roll out the remainder to an oval of the same size and draw a smaller 8 in oval in the center.

2 Brush the edge of the first pastry shape with the beaten egg and place the smaller oval on top. Place on a dampened baking sheet and cook for 30 minutes in the preheated oven.

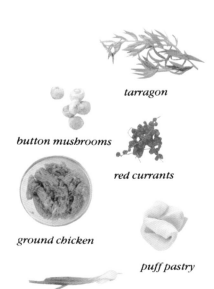

tarragon

button mushrooms

red currants

ground chicken

puff pastry

scallions

3 For the filling, heat the oil in a large pan. Fry the ground chicken for 5 minutes. Add the flour and cook for a further 1 minute. Stir in the milk and stock and bring to a boil.

4 Add the scallions, red currants and mushrooms. Cook for 20 minutes.

5 Stir in the fresh tarragon and season to taste.

VARIATION

You can also use pie crust pastry for this dish and cook as a traditional chicken pie.

6 Place the pastry case on a serving plate, remove the oval center and spoon in the filling. Place the oval lid on top. Serve with freshly cooked vegetables.

Pasta Timbales

An alternative way to serve pasta for a special occasion. Mixed with ground beef and tomato and baked in a lettuce package, it makes an impressive dish for a dinner party.

Serves 4

INGREDIENTS
8 Romaine lettuce leaves

FOR THE FILLING
1 tbsp oil
1½ cups ground beef
1 tbsp tomato paste
1 garlic clove, crushed
¾ cup macaroni
salt and freshly ground black pepper

FOR THE SAUCE
2 tbsp butter
2 tbsp flour
1 cup heavy cream
2 tbsp chopped fresh basil

ground beef

basil

butter

flour

garlic

cream

lettuce

macaroni

tomato paste

1 Preheat the oven to 350°F. For the filling, heat the oil in a large pan and fry the ground beef for 7 minutes. Add the tomato paste and garlic and cook for 5 minutes.

2 Cook the macaroni in boiling water for 8–10 minutes or until *al dente*. Drain.

3 Mix together the pasta and beef.

4 Line four ⅔ cup ramekin dishes with the lettuce leaves. Season the ground beef and spoon into the lettuce-lined ramekins.

5 Fold the lettuce leaves over the beef mixture and place in a roasting pan half-filled with boiling water. Cover and cook for 20 minutes.

6 For the sauce melt the butter in a pan. Add the flour and cook for 1 minute. Stir in the cream and fresh basil. Season and bring to a boil, stirring all the time. Turn out the timbales and serve with the sauce and a crisp green salad.

Fish Bites with Crispy Cabbage

Add an oriental element to a special meal with these attractive and tasty fish bites. Coated in sesame seeds and served with the traditional deep-fried cabbage, they are sure to impress.

Serves 4

INGREDIENTS
FOR THE FISH BITES
12 oz/1½ cups peeled shrimp
12 oz cod fillets
2 tsp light soy sauce
2 tsp sesame seeds
oil for deep-frying

FOR THE CABBAGE
8 oz savoy cabbage
pinch of salt
1 tbsp slivered almonds
soy sauce, to serve

sesame seeds

shrimp

soy sauce

slivered almonds

cod fillets

cabbage

1 Put the shrimp and cod in a food processor and blend for 20 seconds. Place in a bowl and stir in the soy sauce.

2 Roll the mixture into sixteen balls and toss in the sesame seeds to coat.

3 Heat the oil for deep-frying to 325°F. Shred the cabbage and place in the hot oil. Fry for 2 minutes. Drain well and keep warm. Sprinkle the cabbage with salt and toss in the almonds.

4 Fry the balls in two batches for 5 minutes until golden-brown. Remove with a draining spoon. Serve with the cabbage, and soy sauce for dipping.

Ground Beef Wellington

Making use of a popular recipe, this variation retains all the flavors of the original, replacing a joint of expensive cut of meat with a tasty ground beef filling.

Serves 4

INGREDIENTS
FOR THE FILLING
1 tbsp oil
2 lb/8 cups ground beef
1 red onion, chopped
2 garlic cloves, crushed
2 tbsp flour
⅔ cup red wine
2 tbsp chopped fresh oregano
¾ cup wild and long grain rice, mixed
1 egg, beaten

FOR THE PASTRY CASE
1 lb prepared puff pastry
8 oz country pâté
½ cup mixed chopped nuts
beaten egg to glaze
salt and freshly ground black pepper

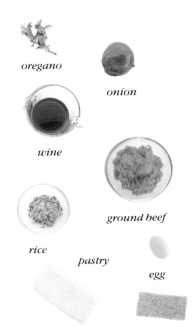

oregano

onion

wine

ground beef

rice

pastry

egg

pâté

1 Preheat the oven to 400°F. For the filling, heat the oil in a pan. Add the ground beef, onion and garlic, and fry for 10 minutes. Stir in the flour and cook for a further 1 minute. Stir in the wine and bring to a boil. Add the oregano and cook for 20 minutes.

2 Cook the rice in boiling salted water for 10 minutes or until *al dente*. Drain well and stir into the beef mixture with the egg. Season to taste and cool.

3 Roll out the pastry to a 14 × 10 in rectangle. Trim the edges and reserve. Place the beef mixture in the center of the pastry along its length. Top with the pâté and nuts.

4 Brush the edges of the pastry with egg and fold around to encase the filling. Turn over and arrange the pastry trimmings in a lattice pattern on top. Brush with the beaten egg and place on a dampened baking sheet. Cook in the preheated oven for 45 minutes. Serve with freshly cooked vegetables.

Filo Pie

Ready-made filo pastry is easy to use and very effective in appearance. Thin sheets of folded pastry encase a lightly spiced, fruity lamb filling to give a tasty and attractive pie.

Serves 4

INGREDIENTS
1 tbsp oil
1 lb/4 cups ground lamb
1 red onion, sliced
2 tbsp chopped fresh cilantro
2 tbsp flour
1¼ cups lamb stock
½ cup canned chick peas, rinsed and drained
1 tsp ground cumin
8 oz filo pastry
1¼ cups ready-to-eat dried apricots
1 zucchini, sliced
2 tbsp melted butter
salt and freshly ground black pepper

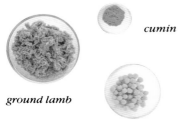

ground lamb

cumin

chick peas

cilantro

apricots

onion

filo pastry

zucchini

1 Preheat the oven to 375°F. Heat the oil in a large pan. Add the ground lamb and cook for 5 minutes. Stir in the onion, fresh cilantro and flour and cook for a further 1 minute.

2 Pour in the stock and chickpeas. Season to taste and stir in the cumin. Cook for 20 minutes.

3 Line a deep ovenproof dish with four sheets of filo pastry.

4 Spoon in the lamb mixture. Top with dried apricots and zucchini.

5 Lay two sheets of filo pastry on top of the filling and brush with the melted butter. Fold the remaining sheets on top. Pour on the remainder of the butter and cook in the oven for 40 minutes. Serve with freshly cooked vegetables.

Chicken Roll

A relatively simple dish to prepare, this recipe uses ground beef as a filling. It is rolled in chicken meat which is spread with a creamy garlic cheese that just melts in the mouth.

Serves 4

INGREDIENTS
4 boneless chicken breasts, about
    4 oz each
4 oz/1 cup ground beef
2 tbsp chopped fresh chives
8 oz creamy garlic cheese
2 tbsp honey
salt and freshly ground black pepper

ground beef

garlic cheese

chicken breast

chives

honey

1 Preheat the oven to 375°F. Place the chicken breasts between two pieces of plastic wrap. Beat with a meat mallet until ¼ in thick and joined together.

2 Place the ground beef in a large pan. Fry for 3 minutes and add the fresh chives and seasoning. Cool.

3 Place the chicken on a board and spread with the cheese.

4 Top with the beef mixture.

5 Roll up the chicken to form a sausage shape.

6 Brush with honey and place in a roasting pan. Cook for 1 hour in the preheated oven. Remove from the pan and slice thinly. Serve with freshly cooked vegetables.

Chow Mein

One of the most well-known Chinese dishes, this recipe is both easy to prepare and healthy.

Serves 4

INGREDIENTS
8 oz dried egg noodles
2 tbsp oil
1 onion, chopped
½ in fresh ginger root, chopped
2 garlic cloves, crushed
2 tbsp soy sauce
¼ cup dry white wine
2 tsp Chinese five-spice powder
1 lb/4 cups ground pork
4 scallions, sliced
2 oz oyster mushrooms
3 oz bamboo shoots
1 tbsp sesame oil
shrimp crackers, to serve

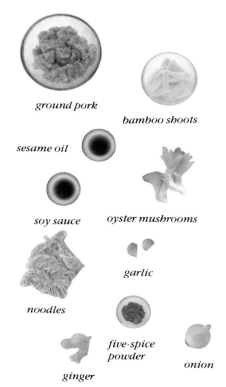

ground pork

bamboo shoots

sesame oil

soy sauce   *oyster mushrooms*

noodles

garlic

five-spice powder   *onion*   *scallions*

ginger

1 Cook the noodles in boiling water for 4 minutes and drain.

2 Meanwhile, heat the oil in a wok and add the onion, ginger, garlic, soy sauce and wine. Cook for 1 minute. Stir in the Chinese five-spice powder.

3 Add the pork and cook for 10 minutes, stirring continuously. Add the scallions, mushrooms, bamboo shoots and continue to cook for a further 5 minutes.

4 Stir in the noodles and sesame oil. Mix all the ingredients together well and serve with shrimp crackers.

Beef Stroganoff

A great standby when entertaining, beef stroganoff is easy to prepare. Simply serve with rice for a quick and very tasty meal.

Serves 4

INGREDIENTS
1 tbsp oil
1 lb/4 cups ground beef
1 onion, quartered
2 tbsp tomato paste
2 tbsp flour
2 cups beef stock
1 green bell pepper, seeded, halved
   and sliced
4 oz mushrooms, sliced
1¼ cups sour cream
salt and freshly ground black pepper
fresh parsley, to garnish

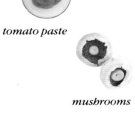

cream

ground beef

pepper

onion

tomato paste

mushrooms

1 Heat the oil in a frying pan. Add the ground beef and cook for 5 minutes. Stir in the onion, tomato paste and flour. Cook for 1 minute.

2 Stir in the beef stock. Season well and bring to a boil.

3 Add the pepper and mushrooms. Cook for a further 20 minutes.

4 Stir in half of the sour cream and cook for 10 minutes. Garnish with fresh parsley and serve with freshly cooked rice and the remaining sour cream.

Cheeseburgers

Loved by all kids, there is nothing to beat a home-made burger. Served with favorite fries in a lightly toasted bun, this burger is bound together with bulghur wheat which is good for them too.

Serves 4

INGREDIENTS
½ cup bulghur wheat
8 oz/2 cups ground beef
1 onion
1 tbsp chopped fresh parsley
1 tbsp tomato paste
1 tbsp freshly grated Parmesan cheese
1 egg beaten
4 hamburger buns
lettuce leaves
4 cheese slices
ketchup
salt and freshly ground black pepper

ground beef

hamburger buns

onion

parsley

egg

bulghur wheat

cheese slices

Parmesan cheese

tomato paste

1 Place the bulghur wheat in a bowl and add enough boiling water to cover. Leave to stand for 10 minutes. Drain off any excess liquid if necessary.

2 Put the ground beef into a bowl and break up with a fork.

3 Place the onion and fresh parsley in a food processor and process for 20 seconds. Add to the beef.

4 Stir in the tomato paste and grated cheese. Season well. Add the drained bulghur wheat.

5 Stir in the beaten egg and bring the mixture together. Shape into four hamburgers with your hands. Broil for 8–10 minutes each side under a medium heat or until cooked through.

COOK'S TIP

Let the kids assemble their own hamburgers and provide alternative relishes and pickles for added interest!

6 Split the hamburger buns in half and place a hamburger inside each one together with some lettuce leaves. Top with a cheese slice and a spoonful of ketchup and the hamburger bun top. Serve with fries and a crisp green salad.

Calzone

This variation on a pizza is bound to be popular. A simple pizza dough encases a tasty ground beef and spinach filling with a tangy cheese sauce.

Serves 4

INGREDIENTS

FOR THE DOUGH
4½ cups self-rising flour
½ cup butter
1 cup milk

FOR THE FILLING
1 tbsp oil
6 oz/1½ cups ground beef
1 tbsp chopped fresh basil
1 onion, sliced
2 tbsp flour
⅔ cup beef stock
4 oz spinach, shredded
beaten egg to glaze
salt and freshly ground black pepper

FOR THE SAUCE
1 tbsp butter
1 tbsp flour
⅔ cup milk
¼ cup freshly grated Parmesan cheese
1 tsp mustard

butter

onion

Parmesan cheese

mustard

ground beef

spinach

1 Preheat the oven to 425°F. For the dough, sift the flour into a bowl. Rub in the butter until the mixture resembles bread crumbs.

2 Stir in the milk and bring the mixture together to form a dough. Cut into four equal pieces and roll each one into a 6 in circle.

3 For the filling, heat the oil in a large pan, add the ground beef and cook for 5 minutes. Stir in the fresh basil and onion. Season to taste and add the flour. Cook for 1 minute. Stir in the stock and bring to a boil. Cook for 10 minutes.

4 Blanch the spinach for 2 minutes and drain well. Place the dough circles on a lightly oiled baking sheet and place the spinach on one half of each circle. Top with the beef mixture.

5 For the sauce, melt the butter and add the flour. Cook for 1 minute. Stir in the milk, cheese and mustard and bring to a boil, stirring all the time.

6 Spoon the sauce onto the beef and spinach. Dampen the edges of the dough with water and fold over to encase the mixtures and form semi-circles. Brush with beaten egg and cook for 20 minutes. Serve with a crisp green salad.

Stuffed Naan

Now widely available, naan breads are growing in popularity. Here, individual breads are warmed and split and used as an alternative to a hamburger bun.

Serves 4

INGREDIENTS
4 oz/1 cup ground beef
4 oz/1 cup pork sausage meat
1 tsp mixed dried herbs
1 tbsp A-1 sauce
4 mini naan breads
4 tbsp mango chutney
salt and freshly ground black pepper

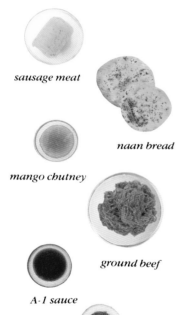

sausage meat

naan bread

mango chutney

ground beef

A-1 sauce

dried herbs

1 Place the ground beef in a bowl and break up with a fork.

2 Add the sausage meat and herbs and season well. Stir in the A-1 sauce.

3 Bring the mixture together with your hands and form into four patties. Broil under a medium heat for 8 minutes, turning once.

4 Place the naan breads under a medium broiler for 2–3 minutes. Split and place the patties and chutney inside. Serve with a crisp green salad.

Bean Bake

This is a variation on a hot-pot. Ground beef combines with baked beans and a tangy barbecue sauce which is topped with slices of potato for a filling, nutritious meal for winter evenings.

Serves 4

INGREDIENTS
2 large potatoes, sliced
1 tbsp oil
12 oz/3 cups ground beef
1 onion, sliced
10 oz can baked beans
6 tbsp barbecue sauce
½ cup freshly grated Gruyère
  cheese
salt and freshly ground black pepper
chopped fresh parsley, to garnish

onion

parsley

Gruyère cheese

barbecue sauce

ground beef

baked beans

potato

I Preheat the oven to 400°F. Cook the potatoes in boiling water for 10 minutes. Drain well and reserve.

2 Heat the oil in a large pan and fry the ground beef and onion for 5 minutes.

VARIATION

If you wish, substitute the baked beans with any canned beans of your choice and replace the barbecue sauce with tomato ketchup.

3 Add the baked beans and barbecue sauce. Season well. Spoon into the base of an ovenproof dish.

4 Arrange the sliced potatoes, overlapping, on top of the beef. Sprinkle with the grated cheese and cook for 30 minutes in the preheated oven. Remove from the oven, sprinkle with the fresh parsley and serve with freshly cooked vegetables.

Beef Pie

This is a really fun-packed meal for the kids. A happy face with hair made of sprouts will encourage any child to eat a good meal.

Serves 4

INGREDIENTS
1 tbsp oil
6 oz/1½ cups ground beef
4 oz large beef sausages
2 tbsp flour
1 × 7 oz can chopped tomatoes
6 tbsp beef stock
2 tbsp chopped fresh parsley
¼ cup tomato ketchup
1 tbsp granulated sugar
11 oz prepared pie crust pastry
beaten egg to glaze
sprouts, to garnish

tomato ketchup

sausages

parsley

sugar

pastry

canned tomato

ground beef

1 Preheat the oven to 375°F. Heat the oil in a large pan and fry the ground beef for 5 minutes.

2 Slice the sausages and add to the pan. Cook for a further 5 minutes. Add the flour and cook for 1 minute.

3 Stir in the chopped tomatoes, stock, fresh parsley, ketchup and sugar. Cook for 10 minutes, stirring occasionally.

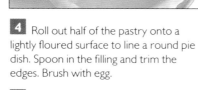

4 Roll out half of the pastry onto a lightly floured surface to line a round pie dish. Spoon in the filling and trim the edges. Brush with egg.

5 Roll out the remaining pastry for the lid. Cut out two "eyes" and a "mouth" and place on top of the pie. Knock up the edges and seal. Brush with beaten egg and cook for 30 minutes in the preheated oven.

VARIATION

This mixture can also be used as the filling for a more adult oriented cottage pie. Just top with mashed potato, sprinkle with grated cheese and cook as before.

6 Remove the pie from the oven and arrange the sprouts around the top of the pie for the "hair". Serve immediately with freshly cooked vegetables.

Popovers

Great fun and full of goodness, these individual corn popovers are filled with tasty meatballs and then baked. Served with salad or baked beans, they will appeal to children everywhere.

Serves 4

INGREDIENTS
FOR THE BATTER
½ cup flour
pinch of salt
1 egg
⅔ cup milk
½ cup canned corn, drained
1 tbsp butter

FOR THE FILLING
4 oz/1 cup ground beef
1 red onion, chopped
2 tbsp tomato sauce
1 cup fresh whole wheat bread crumbs
1 tbsp oil
salt and freshly ground black pepper

bread crumbs

corn

flour

onion

egg

tomato sauce

ground beef

1 Preheat the oven to 425°F. For the batter sift the flour and salt into a bowl. Make a well in the center.

2 Crack the egg and whisk into the flour mixture, add the milk gradually to form a smooth batter. Add the corn.

3 For the filling, place the ground beef in a bowl. Add the onion and seasoning.

4 Stir in the tomato sauce and bread crumbs and bring the mixture together. Roll into four equal-sized balls.

5 Heat the oil in a large pan and fry the meatballs to seal. Place the butter in a four-section popover pan. Put into the preheated oven until melted.

6 Divide the batter between each section of the pan and place a meatball in the center of each. Cook for 30 minutes. Remove from the oven and serve with freshly cooked vegetables or a salad.

Ham and Egg Pots

It is easy to grind any meat to produce quick and economical meals. Here cooked ham is finely ground and cooked in individual dishes with spinach, pineapple and egg for a nutritious meal.

Serves 4

INGREDIENTS
6 oz/1½ cups cooked ham
1 tsp dried thyme
2 tbsp Worcestershire sauce
2 oz spinach, shredded
½ cup crushed canned pineapple
   in natural juice, drained
4 eggs
salt and freshly ground black pepper

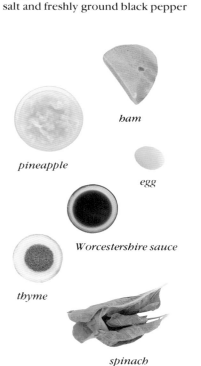

ham

pineapple

egg

Worcestershire sauce

thyme

spinach

1 Preheat the oven to 400°F. Place the ham in a food processor for 30 seconds to grind. Transfer to a bowl and season. Stir in the thyme and Worcestershire sauce.

2 Blanch the spinach in boiling water for 2 minutes. Drain well.

3 Spoon alternate layers of ham, spinach and pineapple into four ⅔ cup ramekin dishes.

4 Top each pot with an egg. Cover with buttered foil and place in a roasting pan half-filled with water. Cook for 20 minutes. Serve with a green salad.

Chili Con Carne

A classic recipe that has become a regular feature in many homes. Simple and economical, it is one of the most popular ground beef recipes developed. This recipe is slightly toned down as children are not generally wild about hot dishes.

Serves 4

INGREDIENTS
1 tbsp oil
8 oz/2 cups ground beef
1 onion, quartered
1 tsp chili powder
2 tbsp flour
2 tbsp tomato paste
⅔ cup beef stock
1 × 7 oz can chopped tomatoes
1 × 7 oz can kidney beans, drained
1 green bell pepper, seeded and
   chopped
1 tbsp Worcestershire sauce
½ cup long grain rice
salt and freshly ground black pepper
sour cream, to serve
chopped fresh parsley, to garnish

canned tomato

pepper

kidney beans

onion

chili powder

rice

ground beef

1 Heat the oil in a large pan and fry the ground beef, onion and chili powder for 7 minutes.

2 Add the flour and tomato paste and cook for 1 minute. Stir in the stock and tomatoes and bring to a boil.

3 Add the kidney beans, green pepper and Worcestershire sauce. Reduce the heat, simmer and continue to cook for 45 minutes.

4 Meanwhile cook the rice in boiling salted water for 10–12 minutes. Drain well. Spoon onto the serving plate. Spoon the chili over the rice, add a spoonful of sour cream and garnish with fresh parsley.

Beef Dough Balls

A great way to use up any leftover pizza dough. The cheese-flavored meatball is surrounded by a light bread case – a new take on a turnover.

Serves 4

INGREDIENTS
FOR THE DOUGH
2 cups self-rising flour
4 tbsp butter
½ cup milk
beaten egg to glaze

FOR THE FILLING
6 oz/1½ cups ground beef
1 tbsp tomato paste
¼ cup frozen peas
¼ cup freshly grated mozzarella
    cheese
salt and freshly ground black pepper

milk

tomato paste

flour

peas

egg

mozzarella cheese

ground beef

butter

1 Preheat the oven to 400°F. For the dough, sift the flour into a bowl. Rub in the butter until the mixture resembles bread crumbs. Gradually stir in the milk to form a dough.

2 Cut the dough into sixteen equal pieces and roll into 4 in circles on a lightly floured surface.

3 For the filling, dry-fry the ground beef for 3 minutes, stirring all the time. Add the tomato paste and peas.

4 Remove the pan from the heat and stir in the grated cheese. Season well.

5 Spoon the mixture into the center of each dough circle. Dampen the edges of the dough and bring to the centre, folding around to encase the beef mixture. Pinch together at the top.

6 Carefully re-shape into balls and place on an oiled baking sheet. Cook in the preheated oven for 20 minutes. Serve with a crunchy salad.